Cincinnati Art Museum
June 29 through September 1, 1985

Quilts

from Cincinnati Collections

Copyright 1985 Cincinnati Art Museum
All rights reserved. Printed in the United States of America.

The Museum gratefully acknowledges operational
support from the Cincinnati Fine Arts Fund,
the Ohio Arts Council and the Institute of Museum Services.

Designer: Noel Martin
Typesetter: Cobb Typesetting Co.
Printer: Young & Klein Inc.
Photography: Ron Forth

Cincinnati Art Museum, Eden Park, Cincinnati, Ohio 45202

ISBN 0-931537-02-9

Quilting—*the stitching together of several layers of textiles—has a very long history, the word itself deriving from the Latin word for a stuffed sack. One of the brightest chapters in that long history flowered in the United States in the late eighteenth and particularly the nineteenth centuries.*

The European settlers of North America brought the techiques with them and used those techniques to produce bedcovers that were as beautiful as they were useful. They were so universally appealing that quilts were made in great numbers, many of them surviving today and commanding increasing respect as an art form. Quilts are folk art at its finest—not taught in art schools but spread by emulation among friends and handed down the generations, usually from mother to daughter, though sometimes men participated. They exhibit a cumulative excellence of design sense executed with the most refined craftsmanship which transcends the passage of time. In contemporary hands, pieced, stitched and stuffed fabric compositions have escaped from domestic service and are being created for display on walls without first doing duty as bedcovers.

There is no need to review here the history and techniques of quilt making which have been thoroughly covered in the dozens of books on the subject already on the market. This catalogue is intended simply to provide a lasting record of quilts that are ordinarily seen by only a handful of people, those in the Museum's collection being seldom exhibited because of their space requirements, and those in the hands of private collectors being seen only by their friends.

A few of the works in this exhibition, notably the Crazy Patchwork and the Adam and Eve appliqué, are not really quilts at all since they are neither stuffed nor quilted, but they are so closely related aesthetically and technically to the true quilts that they have been accorded honorary status as quilts and have been included in the exhibition.

Dimensions are given in inches, height before width. Quilts from the Museum's collection can be recognized by the donor's name and accession number at the end of the description. Quilts borrowed for the exhibition are identified by the lenders' names.

The Museum is very grateful to the private collectors who have contributed so significantly to the success of the exhibition by lending their treasures, and it is perhaps permissible to hope that lenders will turn into donors at some time in the future.

Thanks are due Noel Martin for the design of this catalogue and Ron Forth for the photography. Kathryn L. Taulbee, Registrar, and Mary Ellen Goeke, Assistant Registrar, helped assemble the borrowed quilts, and preparation of the quilts for exhibition was performed by an enthusiastic squad of volunteers: Mrs. Barbara McGill, Mrs. William D. Meyer, Mrs. Gerald Osterman, Irene Phelps, Marie Pressler, Mrs. Julius Sanks, Mrs. John E. Schmidt, Mrs. William Strybel, Mrs. Chester Sudbrack, Jr. and Mrs. Warren Walker

Carolyn R. Shine, Curator
Costume, Textiles and Tribal Arts

1.

Framed Center Hewson Print. Made by Betsy (Mrs.
Robert) Burton (initials B.B. stitched on either side of lip of
vase), great-grandmother of donor, Sussex County,
Delaware, dated 1811 (stitched below vase), pieced cottons,
92 x 90. The center block-printed vase of flowers is
attributable to John Hewson, a Philadelphia textile printer,
on the basis of documented examples in the Philadelphia
Museum of Art. Published: Orlofsky, p. 46; *On View,* Vol.
9, 1975, p. 64; Bishop, p. 24; Bullard and Shiell, p. 17;
Kobayashi, p. 27. Gift of Mary Louise Burton. 1973.400.

2.

Adam and Eve in the Garden. Unidentified maker,
American or English, late 18th or early 19th century,
applied cotton figures, plants, animals, etc., cross stitch
inscriptions partly disintegrated: "… know…" "And she
gave also unto her husband with her and he did eat."
"Adam," "Eve," 55½ x 45¾. Bequest of
Mrs. W. M. Simmons. 1965.280.

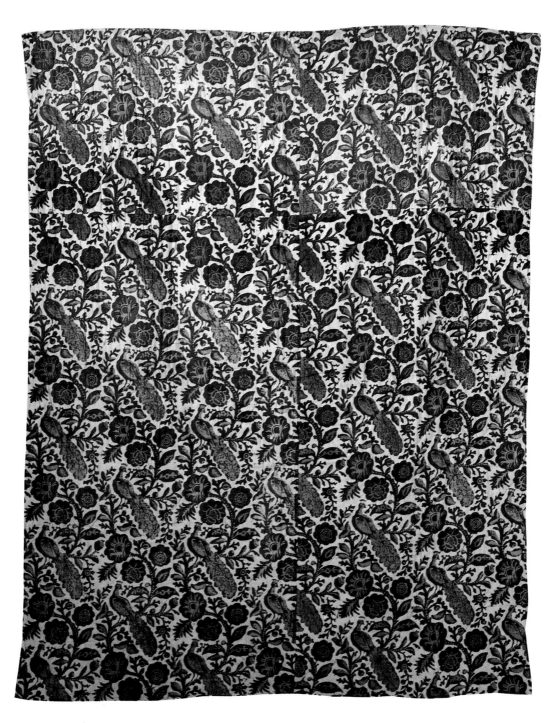

3.

Blue and White Resist Print. Unidentified maker, handed down in the family of donor's maternal grandmother, the Drews, who lived in Albany, New York, during the Revolution, then between Brewster and Carmel, New York, then Connecticut, late 18th or early 19th century, resist printed and indigo dyed cotton, pieced front and back to make whole cloth, cotton filling, 85¾ x 67¾. Gift of Ruth Dalrymple. 1983.299.

4.

Crewel Embroidered Center. Unidentified maker, the
crewel embroidered linen center may date from the 18th
century, the quilted printed cotton drops have three blue
threads in the selvage signifying English origin between
1774 and 1811, wool filling, 96½ x 94. Published: Safford
and Bishop, p. 67; Bishop, p. 28 (incorrectly credited to
Greenfield Village). Gift of Mrs. Arthur Holmes Morse.
1944.91.

5.

Center Medallion. Made by Mrs. Charlotte Dabney, probably early 19th century, applied center basket of flowering branches and birds, anchors and garlands cut from various late 18th and early 19th century printed cottons, 103 x 98½. Published: Safford and Bishop, p. 174. Gift of Lou Gaddis. 1912.252.

6.

White Trapunto. Made by Sarah J. Kelley (stitched at base of flower basket), great, great-aunt of donor, 1856 (stitched at bases of both flower and fruit baskets), "E Pluribus Unum" stitched in central eagle's banderole, cotton, 87 x 87. Gift of James G. Headley. 1981.470.

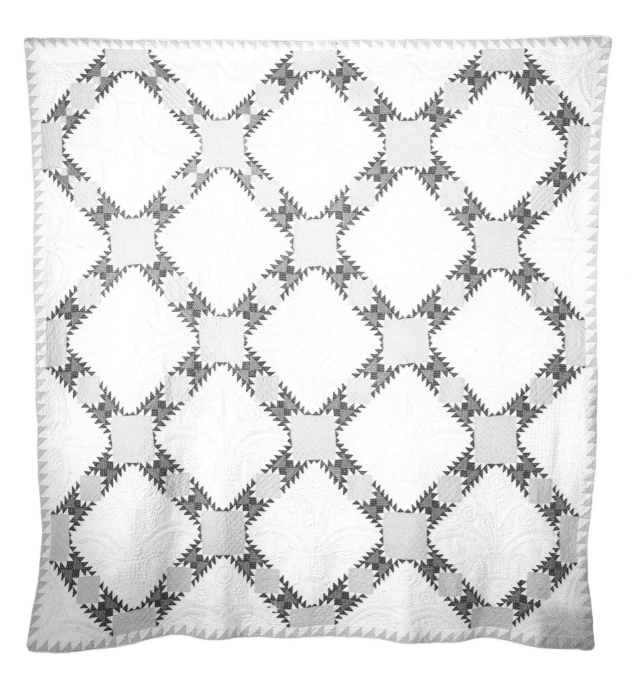

7.
Feathered Square or **Feathered Cross.** Made by Sarah
M. L. (stitched and stuffed in border), probably Sarah
M. Lail, probably second half of 19th century, cottons
pieced and stuffed, 86 x 84. Published: Orlofsky, pp. 123,
286. Gift of Mrs. William Lail. 1972.365.

8.
Mariner's Compass or **Sunbursts.** Unidentified
maker, probably mid-19th century, cottons pieced, applied
and stuffed, 87¼ x 85¼. Published: Orlofsky, p. 322. Gift
of Mary Hutton Baker and Elizabeth Hutton Baker.
1942.85.

9.

Mosaic or **Grandmother's Flower Garden.** Made by
Amelia Emilina Wilson, handed down in the Boswell
family, Cincinnati, probably 19th century, wool, pieced, 91 x
78. Published: Bishop, p. 36. Gift of Mrs. J. Arthur Buhr in
the name of William P. Boswell and Frances Boswell
Lambert. 1962.499.

10.

Log Cabin, Courthouse Steps. Made by Mary
Elizabeth Overall Johnston, Louisville, Kentucky, born
1836, grandmother of donor, probably second half of 19th
century, silks and silk ribbon, 75 x 71½. Gift of Mrs. Harold
Brownfield. 1967.1159.

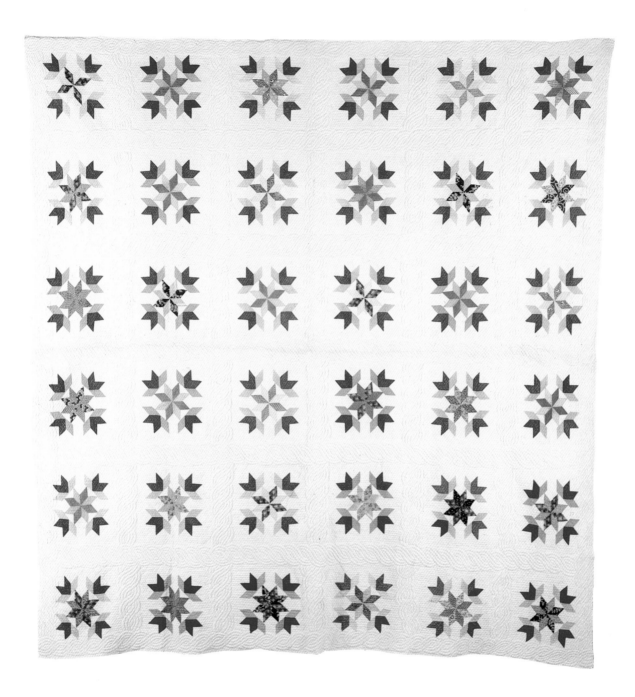

11.

Blazing Star. Unidentified maker, probably 19th
century, cottons pieced and stuffed, 93 x 93. Gift of Mrs.
E. B. Patterson. 1933.26.

12.

Crazy Patchwork. Made by the mother or grandmother
of the donor, after 1888 (one patch is a souvenir ribbon of
the Ohio Valley Centennial dated 1888), silks, velvets and
ribbons joined by embroidery, 69 x 69. Published:
McMorris, *Quilting*, WBGU-TV, Program 11; McMorris,
Crazy Quilts, Fig. 93. Gift of Edna Pearl Cotteral. 1967.185.

13.

Peonies. Made by Kate and Eunice Langdon, great-aunts of donor, Cincinnati, probably about 1900, cottons pieced and applied, 101 x 88. Gift of Mary Louise Burton. 1973.418.

14.

Geometric Album. Made by Mary Caroline Woolley
Smith and her granddaughter Elizabeth Smith Wilson
(Mrs. Russell), Cincinnati, between 1848 and 1949, the
colored cottons applied on the white patches which are
inscribed with the names of relatives and friends, the
earliest dated 1848 and the latest 1949 when Mrs. Wilson
assembled the blocks and had them quilted at the Cincinnati
Woman's Exchange, 94 x 87½. Published: Bishop, p. 53.
Gift of Mrs. Russell Wilson. 1972.106.

15.

The Cincinnati Quilt. Made by Barbara Beebe, Myra Boles, Eileen Bowen, Linda M. Britton, Judy Dobler, Fran Ewing, Dot Flick, Miriam Flick, Victoria B. Foken, Jane Goodrich, Sue Hurst, Charlotte Kielborth, Sandra Manteuffel, Ferne Mason, Lynne McGlade, Pauline Minder, Hattie Morris, Carolyn O'Bryan, Pat Scholten, Hildred Schouse, Susan Wolven, Sheila Wolson, Aloyse Yorko and Marilyn Zeh (names embroidered on individual blocks), Cincinnati, 1973 (embroidered on blocks), mixed materials, 114 x 90, applied scenes of Cincinnati made in an adult quilting class at Anderson Township High School taught by Betty Jane Alfers, and presented to the City of Cincinnati. Published: *Cincinnati Enquirer*, April 9, 1974, p. 17; *Cincinnati Magazine*, March 1975, pp. 30-33; McMorris, *Quilting*, WBGU-TV, Program 8. Lent by the City of Cincinnati. 45.1974.

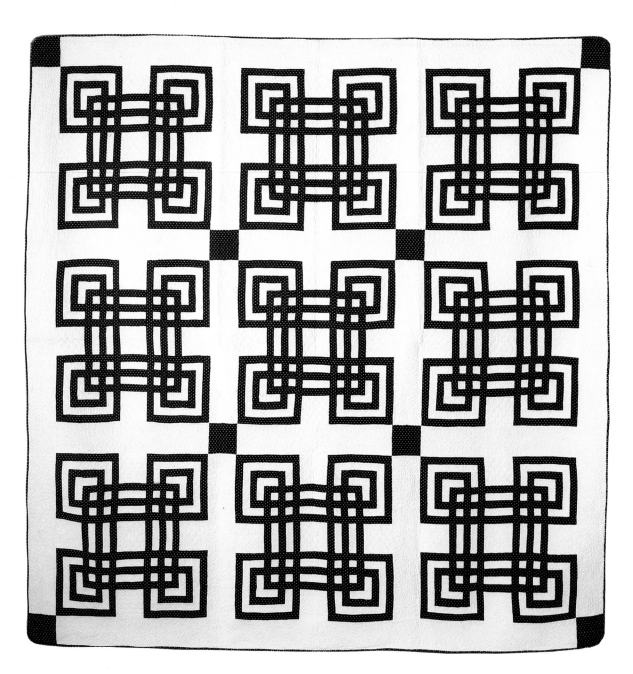

16.

Carpenter's Square or **Gordion Knot.** Unidentified maker, handed down in the Battin family, Columbiana County, Ohio, probably mid-19th century, pieced cottons, 80 x 80. Lent by Mr. and Mrs. Dalton Battin.

17.
Ivy Leaf Variation. Unidentified maker, handed down in
the Battin family, Columbiana County, Ohio, probably
mid-19th century, pieced cottons, 81 x 81. Lent by Mr. and
Mrs. Dalton Battin.

18.

Feathered Star. Made by lender's grandmother Rebecca
Cook Ter Bush (Mrs. Charles Ter Bush), 1831-1902
(stamped Rebecca C. Bush), Morton, New York, made after
1882 when the Bush house burned down, applied and pieced
cottons, 95 x 80. Lent by Mrs. Samuel M. Blakemore.

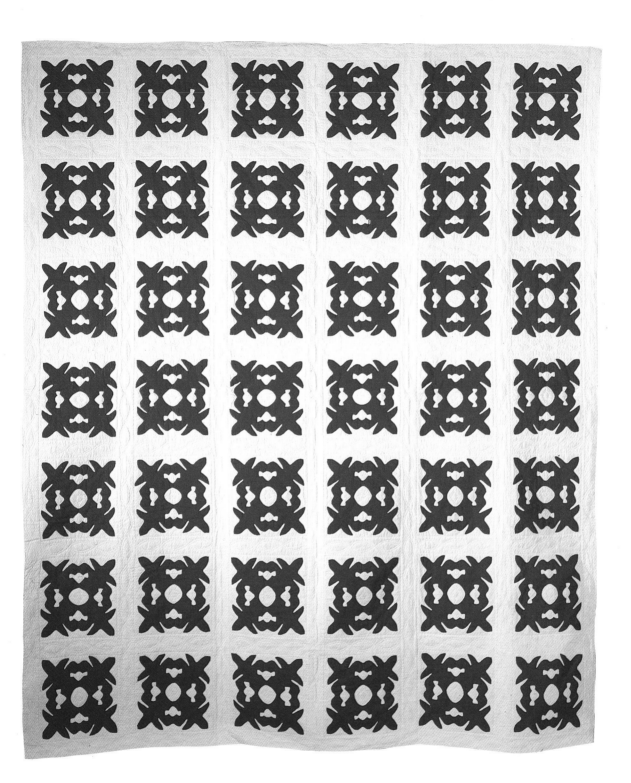

19.

Oak Leaf Variation. Made by the women's auxiliary of the First Dutch Reformed Church, Preakness, New Jersey, for lender's grandfather, the Rev. Benjamin Van Doren Wyckoff, about 1879-80, applied cottons, 93 x 82½. Lent by Ruth Dalrymple.

20.

Rising Star. Made by the Ohio Valley Quilters' Guild,
1984, pieced cottons, 102 x 89. Lent by Dr. Peter St.J. Dignan.

21.

Borders to a Square. Unidentified maker, probably New
England, early 19th century, pieced cottons, 100 x 97. Lent
by Federation Antiques.

22.

Stars and Plumes or **Princess Feather.** Unidentified maker, handed down in the family of Claud Bruner, Washington Court House, Ohio, who married lender's aunt, applied cottons, 95 x 95. Lent by Mrs. Russell Flee.

23.

Sunburst Variation. Family records state that this was made by Anne Newman, probably of Rising Sun, Indiana, great, great-grandmother of lender, early 19th century, pieced cottons, 84 x 89. Lent by Margaret Hall.

24.

October Moonrise. Made by Barbara B. Hester (Mrs.
Philip G.), Harrison, Ohio, 1983, pieced cottons, 84 x 84.
Lent by Barbara B. Hester.

25.

Mosaic (unfinished). Made by Frances Schillinger,
Cincinnati, great-grandmother of Mr. Hopple, pieced silks,
53 x 44. Lent by Mr. and Mrs. William H. Hopple, Jr.

26.

Deer Dancers of San Ildefonso. Made by Terrie
Mangat (Mrs. D. S.), Cincinnati, 1983, pieced and applied
textiles, sequins, quills, etc., 105 x 105. Published: *House
Beautiful*, January 1985, pp. 78-79. Lent by Terrie Mangat.

27.
Winter's End. Made by Carolyn Muller (Mrs. D. C.),
1982, pieced and applied cottons, silks, etc., 63 x 60. Lent by
Carolyn Muller.

28.

Oak Leaves and Acorns. Unidentified maker, handed
down in Mr. Murphy's family, the Buxtons, Cincinnati,
probably 19th century, applied cottons, 101 x 80. Lent by
Mr. and Mrs. Rufus W. Murphy.

29.

Young Man's Fancy. Unidentified maker, handed down in Mr. Murphy's family, the Buxtons, Cincinnati, probably 19th century, pieced cottons, 82 x 68. Lent by Mr. and Mrs. Rufus W. Murphy.

30.

Star of Bethlehem or **Star of Texas.** Family records
state that this was pieced by E. S. Clarke, Monroeville,
Alabama, great-aunt of Mrs. Palmer, in 1849, and quilted
by a slave, Aunt Peggy, of Burnt Corn, Alabama, pieced
cottons, 104 x 104. Lent by Mr. and Mrs. Cletus T. Palmer.

31.
Nine Sunny Days. Made by Elaine Plogman, (Mrs.
Robert L.), Cincinnati, 1983, pieced cottons, 63 x 63. Lent
by Elaine Plogman.

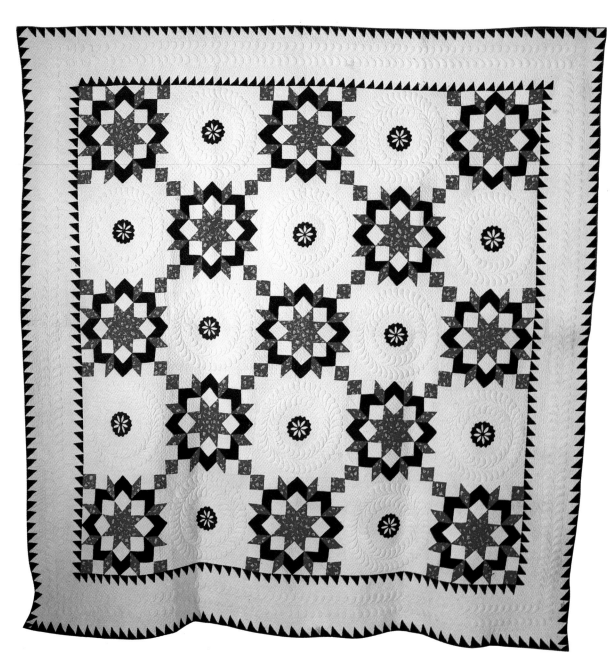

32.

Broken Star. Unidentified maker, attached card says
came "from Aunt Anne White – Avella, Pa., in 1932,
approximately 125 years old – made by great gr White,"
pieced cottons, stuffed, 85 x 85. Lent by Madeline Smith
and Jolly Gardeners Antiques.

33.
Feathered Star. Unidentified maker, probably 19th
century, pieced cottons, 90 x 90. Lent by Madeline Smith
and Jolly Gardeners Antiques.

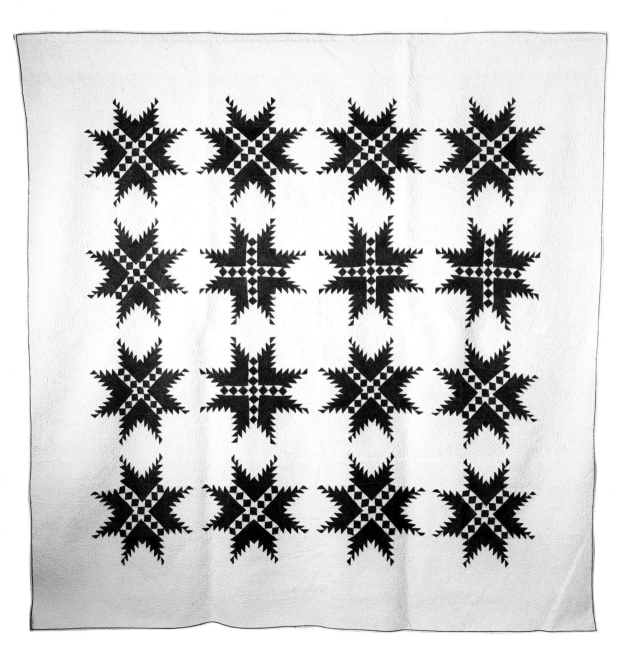

Bibliography

Bishop, Robert, *New Discoveries in American Quilts*, New York, E. P. Dutton and Co., 1975.

Bullard, Lacy and Betty Jo Schiell, *Chintz Quilts: Unfading Glory*, Tallahassee, Florida, Serendipity Publishers, 1983.

Kobayashi, Kei, *A Loving Study of American Patchwork Quilts*, Japan, Bunka, 1983.

McMorris, Penny, *Quilting*, Bowling Green, Ohio, WBGU-TV, 1981.

McMorris, Penny, *Crazy Quilts*, New York, E. P. Dutton and Co., 1984.

On View, London, Plaistow.

Orlofsky, Patsy and Myron, *Quilts in America*, New York, McGraw Hill Book Company, 1974.

Safford, Carleton and Robert Bishop, *America's Quilts and Coverlets*, New York, E. P. Dutton and Co., 1972.